A Stingray Bit My Nipple!

A Stingray Bit My Nipple!

True Stories from Real Travelers

Erik Torkells and the Readers
of Budget Travel.

Andrews McMeel
Publishing, LLC

Kansas City

08 09 10 11 12 WKT 10 9 8 7 6 5 4 3 2

ISBN-13: 978-0-7407-7121-7
ISBN-10: 0-7407-7121-3

Library of Congress Control Number: 2007934962

www.andrewsmcmeel.com

ATTENTION: SCHOOLS AND BUSINESSES

Andrews McMeel books are available at quantity discounts with bulk purchase for educational, business, or sales promotional use. For information, please write to: Special Sales Department, Andrews McMeel Publishing, LLC, 4520 Main Street, Kansas City, Missouri 64111.

Introduction

Every traveler knows: The best memories come from moments when your trip is less than postcard-perfect. Like that time in South Africa when an impala tried to hump you. Or when your hair caught on fire in a church in Venice. Or when a stingray in Grand Cayman spit in your face—or worse, bit your nipple….

As we say in every issue of *Budget Travel* magazine, "Travel is stranger, funnier, and more heartwarming than fiction"—and nothing proves it like the anecdotes in our True Stories section, the best of which have been collected in this book.

Readers often say that True Stories is their favorite part of the magazine. As the editor, I'm not supposed to have a favorite section—but truth be told, mine is True Stories, too. I just get such a kick out of how people are willing not only to laugh at themselves, but also to allow themselves to be laughed at. When we travel, we aim for the sublime. It's the ridiculous stuff, however, that we tend to treasure the most.

Erik Torkells

She's got trunk in the junk

In the jungles of Nepal's Royal Chitwan National Park, my friend and I were invited to bathe with an elephant in the river that flowed directly in front of our guesthouse. The guesthouse owner told me to grab the elephant's ear with my left hand and the other ear with my right hand. Then he smoothed out the elephant's trunk so it curved downward, ending near my feet. "Step on its trunk and it'll flip you onto its back," he said. I grasped the animal's rough, hairy ears and placed one trembling foot on its trunk. Next thing I knew, my crotch was smothering the elephant's face! My friends were too busy laughing to offer any help.

Anna Wexler Cambridge, Mass.

Yeah, if Muppets had two-inch claws

In Panama, while driving from Panama City to the coast, my wife and I crossed paths with a three-toed sloth that decided it needed to cross the road. As we watched it slowly make progress (and that's being generous), we opted to give the Muppet-like creature a hand. After cautiously carrying the sloth across the highway, we said our good-byes and continued our drive looking for wildlife on the Pan-American Highway.

Jacob Jones Poulsbo, Wash.

"i h8 these shoes.
c u 2moro"

My fiancée and I happened upon two beautiful geishas in traditional garb standing outside a temple in Kyoto, Japan. We were commenting on how exciting it was to see them when all of a sudden they stopped talking to each other, pulled cell phones out from their kimonos, and started sending text messages to their friends!

Donny Chu Alameda, Calif.

So that's where Dad is

Requesting information for our visit, my husband was e-mailing the North Fort Myers Chamber of Commerce when the spell-checker questioned the word *accommodations*. Not noticing his mouse slip, he chose *abominations* to replace it. The reply made us laugh: "Thank you for inquiring about the best kept vacation secret in Florida. . . . I guess the only abomination we have is a crusty old man who continues to fish off the bridge downtown in his long johns. But we are working with him. Do come and enjoy!"

Sheree Hobson Portland, Ore.

It's called squeezing the opportunity

In the Algarve region of Portugal, my husband and I encountered three old men on a park bench. I wanted a photo, so I sat between them and tried to make conversation, indicating that we were from Detroit, Michigan, the U.S.—anything they might recognize. The man next to me began speaking Portuguese and then placed a hand on my chest. I listened until I felt that I could politely walk away. Afterward, my husband asked if we should offer them something for being photographed. "No," I replied, "I think they've been duly compensated."

Sue Foote **Harrison Township, Mich.**

Ah, the silver anniversary

We decided to go without hotel reservations while touring France for three weeks for our 25th wedding anniversary. This was no problem until a Friday night in Provence. Finally, we gave up searching for a room and simply asked the proprietor of La Petite Auberge if we could sleep in our car in her parking lot. Aghast, she insisted we stay for dinner while she created suitable accommodations. The staff hauled a rug, a foam mattress, and bedding to her gravel-floored garage. The hospitality was so endearing that we stayed a second night (in one of the conventional rooms).

Cyndee Boyvey and Al Brown **Seminole, Fla.**

He's probably never even seen one

I met a pair of Iranian men—a businessman and his translator—while inside a store in China. "You look like an Iranian woman," the translator said. "Well, thank you," I replied, not exactly sure how to react. "I'll take that as a compliment." Looking me up and down, he said, "No, don't."

Joelle Broberg Littleton, Colo.

Short people got no business taking photos

Upon completing a round of golf in Chiang Mai, Thailand, I asked my playing partner's caddy if she'd take a photo of my caddy and me. Neither caddy spoke English, and both were under five feet tall. This is how the photo turned out.

Glenn F. Tonoli Hacienda Heights, Calif.

One kava, two kava, three kava, floor!

"Try it, you'll like it." That's what the taxi driver in Fiji told my husband and me about kava. Made from pepper plants and served in coconuts, the mildly euphoric drink is served at Fijian ceremonies and social gatherings. Our driver also suggested we drink it at the village chief's house. Upon entering, we found him lying on the floor, apparently so drunk on kava that he couldn't get up for a photo.

Ricki Moyer Lanoka Harbor, N.J.

"And tonight I'd like absolutely nothing at all"

After losing 20 pounds, I considered it safe to take another cruise, but the food and service on Celebrity's *Infinity* were so fantastic that I could feel my waistline expanding with every meal. On the fourth night, I decided to cut out all desserts. Our waiter, however, was incredulous when I said I wanted nothing for dessert. After serving the rest of the table, he brought me a plate with NOTHING written on it in chocolate. I licked up every bit.

Stephanie Pincson San Francisco, Calif.

It's a small, cruel world

In Athens, at the Parthenon, my husband and I asked two women if they'd take our photo. When the women identified themselves as Michiganders, my husband responded that he'd grown up there, in Rochester. "That's where I'm from," said one. She said that she was an elementary school teacher—to which my husband happily replied that his brother is an elementary school principal in Rochester, and offered up his brother's name. "Sure, I know him," she said. "He just fired me."

Janis Townsend **North Caldwell, N.J.**

"So we ate it for lunch"

On a recent cruise to Grand Cayman, we went to Stingray City. As the stingrays swarmed around us, our guide explained how tame they are and offered to lift one so that we could pet it. We all laughed at the friendly smile of the stingray as we took photographs of it. I suppose it had enough of our attention, or I snapped one too many pictures, because it spit salt water right in my face.

Susan Dodder Hattiesburg, Miss.

Our special place is in Vermont

A club in Lima was showcasing Peruvian music and dancing, and I was impressed—until I was pulled onstage to perform the *alcatraz*, a dance where you stick a piece of paper on your partner's behind and try to light it with a candle. To avoid humiliation (and second-degree burns), she must blow the candle out by shaking her booty. I took enjoyment in trying to light my partner, a teacher for the Peruvian National Ballet. When the tables were turned, however, I not only had her candle to contend with, but two others: The other performers stuck their candles in my special place. Their motive was simple: There was a crowd; a blue-eyed, red-headed American; and many cameras.

Jeremy Spencer **Albuquerque, N.M.**

He was just showing off his "WWJD" bracelet

Moving from California to Washington, D.C., after college was a big step for me, so I figured I'd drive cross-country and discover what lies between the two coasts. My best friend and I packed up a big brown van and headed east. In Oklahoma, we saw a bumper sticker that said HONK IF YOU LOVE JESUS. Excited to see some authentic Bible action in the Bible Belt, I honked the horn with zeal. The driver rolled down his window and gave us the finger.

Stina Skewes-Cox Washington, D.C.

Or maybe she's a saint

My girlfriend Shannon and I were at Santa Maria della Salute in Venice. The church offered several different sizes of candles; Shannon picked the tallest, which cost $1. She whipped around to light it without noticing the already-lit candles behind her—and her hair, in a heavily hair-sprayed pony-tail, turned into a bright-red ball of flames. I ran over and pounded her head until I put out the flames. Needless to say, we headed out the door pronto! I asked later if she had paid for the candle. "Well, yes," she said, "but I didn't have a dollar so I put in 50 cents." To which I replied, "And that's why God let only half of your head burn!"

Paula VanDalen **Redington Beach, Fla.**

People in Birkenstocks shouldn't throw stones

"I think that's Selarón," said my brother-in-law about a man at the Selarón Staircase in Rio de Janeiro. I scoffed because he hadn't previously even heard of the Chilean artist. We said hello—it *was* Selarón! We talked for an hour and bought paintings, which he signed. "I'm so embarrassed," said our friend Jane as we left. "I framed the first photo I took so the scruffy guy wouldn't be in it!"

Mary Sienko Minneapolis, Minn.

Only her best friends get to call her that

In Thailand I came down with dengue fever and had to check in to a guesthouse for a few weeks. The innkeeper introduced herself as what I understood to be "So." She took great care of me, and we became friends. When the time came for me to leave, she sat me down and explained that I hadn't been calling her by her real name at all. I'd been using the wrong emphasis and tone, and had really been calling her "Three-Colored Pork."

Samantha Kersten Ham Lake, Minn.

Gene Simmons, your flight is now boarding

I was in Costa Rica when a bad fish meal landed me in bed for two days. The urge to brush my teeth was strong—until I saw my jet-black tongue in the mirror. I raced to the pharmacy, fearing this was a symptom of some dreaded disease. The pharmacists burst out laughing. They asked if I'd been drinking Coke, and, indeed, it was the only thing I drank while in bed. Evidently the levels of tannic acid in Costa Rican Coke are different from what I was used to and had turned my tongue a scary shade of black. When I brushed my teeth, the black—and my fear of disease—vanished.

Todd Ramquist Antioch, Ill.

Reason #2 not to eat bugs

In the Oaxaca market, I spotted a woman with a basket of *chapulines*, the tiny dried grasshoppers that are a popular snack in this part of Mexico. A fellow shopper asked in broken English if I had ever tasted them. I replied that I hadn't, and he bought a small cup. He popped a handful in his mouth and passed the cup to me. You know how a popcorn kernel gets caught in your throat? I had grasshoppers stuck there for the rest of the day.

Megan Dorr **Moran, Wyo.**

That, or your husband has some explaining to do

My husband and I booked a cabin in an eco-resort in Belize. When we arrived, there were chickens running loose around the grounds. The owner told us that they were his insect exterminators. That night we kept all of our windows open, and in the early morning, I heard a chicken squawking close by—*very* close. She was in our bed! And she loved being petted. When we got up, we discovered that she'd even laid an egg.

Thea Platt Shelburne, Vt.

For a good time, call Yertle at 555-1321

Sailing around Panama's San Blas archipelago, I was approached each morning by Kuna Indians in canoes selling lobsters, crabs, and fish. One day they had a 50-pound sea turtle, which they hoped to sell as food. We agreed on a price of $20 and transferred the turtle to my dinghy. When the Kuna were out of sight, I took a Magic Marker and drew a heart on the turtle's back—it was Valentine's Day—along with my name and phone number, and drove it out to the reef and released it.

Sam Leming Indianapolis, Ind.

He was saving it for later

I took my kids, Daniel and Julia, to Walt Disney World when they were four and seven. They were most excited about the plane ride, their first. Before we took off, I gave Daniel a piece of gum and said, "Chew this. It'll help your ears." About 30 seconds later, I was surprised to see him attempting to put his chewed gum inside his ear.

Jean Dehne Whitefish Bay, Wis.

Even better than a genie

Walking Oregon's Tillamook Spit, we discovered a barnacle-encrusted Suntory brandy bottle sealed with wax. Inside were six pieces of damp paper with Japanese characters on them. We contacted a Japanese teacher in Portland and learned that eight fifth-grade boys from Fukuoka had launched the bottle from Okinawa four years earlier—it was part of a ceremony honoring 300 Japanese youths who drowned in 1945 when their evacuation ship was sunk by a U.S. submarine. Having read about my story in the *Portland Oregonian*, a Delta Air Lines representative asked if my wife and I would fly (for free) on Delta's inaugural flight from Oregon to Fukuoka to meet the boys and their families. We happily obliged, and we were treated like royalty at the Grand Hyatt Fukuoka. We visited homes under the glare of TV cameras, and the trip was capped off by an official presentation of the bottle to the suburb of Kasuya on National Culture Day. The bottle is now on display at the Kasuya civic center, with the boys' notes framed alongside it.

John Frewing Tigard, Ore.

So the giraffe says, "Wanna neck?"

The giraffes we encountered at a Kenyan reserve will eat from your hand, but if you put a nugget of food in your mouth, they'll take it from there, too. My grandson Andrew was eager to give it a try—and he got the best kiss of all. French, anyone?

Aileen Saunders College Place, Wash.

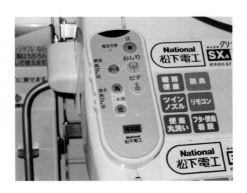

Purple means frappé

In Japan, on my first Asian business trip, I excused myself from a meeting to use the restroom. I looked for the handle to flush, but instead saw a keypad labeled in Japanese. I pondered the situation for at least a minute, and then chose a button. A jet of water from inside the bowl sprayed all over my shirt and tie. With nowhere to move in the tiny stall, I pressed buttons frantically until the water stopped. I soaked up as much of the water as I could with paper towels, and then I made my way back to the meeting, my shirt very wet and my face very red. My polite Japanese hosts continued the meeting without a word about my issues. That evening, over a few drinks, I learned that I wasn't the first Westerner to press the wrong button.

Dave Blake **Chandler, Ariz.**

In other words, you plus-size

My buddy and I were sitting on a bench at our Acapulco hotel when I noticed a Mexican family—father, mother, and seven daughters—smiling at us. The father came over and said, "My oldest daughter would like to take a picture with you." I was confused but said yes. The older girls were beautiful. Soon he had all of his daughters around me, with the two youngest on my lap. When he was finished, each girl shook my hand and thanked me. I was still puzzled—until the father shook my hand and said, "You Pavarotti."

Kenneth Aniballi Dundee, Ill.

Hey, there's more than one way to crack a smile

When I arrived to do the Zorb—a plastic ball that rolls downhill with a person strapped inside—in Rotorua, New Zealand, there was a loudspeaker announcement that, in honor of National Nude Day, anyone who would Zorb naked could go for free. Most of the Zorbers, myself included, chose to wear swimsuits—but standing on the viewing platform was a man completely naked except for hiking socks and boots. He was straight-faced, as if it were the most normal thing in the world.

Jim Caceres **Yonkers, N.Y.**

Probably Jovan Musk

While in South Africa, I went on several game drives, and I think it may have been mating season. Or maybe this one impala was just really lonely. Whatever the case, the animal was quite excited to see Jacob, one of my companions. "Get it off me!" he yelled. "Get it off me!" Our group was laughing so hard that we couldn't help him out. Besides, the impala clearly wasn't going to hurt him. It just wanted to love him. So we kept asking, "What kind of cologne are you wearing, Jacob?"

Sheila Siegel Belleville, Ill.

Cigarettes?
What cigarettes?

Thirty-five years after serving in Vietnam, I returned to visit the places I used to patrol. One day, near the Cambodian border, I heard a noise on the trail leading to the road. All of a sudden, out popped a woman smuggling cigarettes across the border. It was the best laugh of the day.

Tom Layman Petersburg, Mich.

No more coffee for him

I was standing in front of the Jean Tinguely and Niki de Saint Phalle Fountain in Paris, waiting for my wife to take my picture. She looked through the viewfinder, waited a few seconds, and then put the camera down. She lifted the camera again, then put it down again. This happened several times, and I wondered what the problem was. Finally, she snapped a picture. With an aggravated look, she handed me the camera. "Every time I was about to take the photo, a man would jump up and down, wave, and make funny faces!" she said. "He really wanted to be in our picture!"

John Verbrugge **Grand Rapids, Mich.**

Who said anything about getting off?

Having haggled for more than an hour for a camel ride around the pyramids outside Cairo, I felt exceedingly proud that I had gotten my stubborn guide's $20 price reduced by half. Afterward, I patiently waited for the guide to cue the camel to lower me down. Tired of the delay, I asked him if he would let me down—to which he replied, "Ten dollars to ride on camel, ten dollars to get off!"

Suzanne Murrell **Orlando, Fla.**

And 30 minutes later, it was hungry again

On a business trip to China, my associate and I were really hoping to go diving in the South China Sea, so we dragged our scuba gear halfway around the world. In Hong Kong, the night before the dive, I called to confirm our departure—only to hear, in a pleasant but heavily accented voice, "Boat no go out." I couldn't believe it! "Whaddya mean boat no go out?" I said, sharing some of my heated Southern accent in return. "Boat no go out," she replied. "Shok eat customa."

Cliff Slinkard Hogeye, Ark.

Only in first class, mister

I was working as a flight attendant on a flight from Islip, N.Y., to Fort Lauderdale when the call signal from the lavatory chimed several times. I knocked and asked if the occupant was okay when, to my astonishment, he opened the door. He was sitting on the toilet with his pants down. "Miss," he said, "can you get me a golf magazine?"

Vanessa Lynch **Elizabeth, N.J.**

Better him than you

A few days after flying to Australia, my wife and I were in the Blue Mountains, waiting for the cable car at Scenic World. We couldn't wait to see our first koala—and there he was, up in a tree. As we admired this legendarily lethargic creature, we finally noticed that he wasn't moving at all. That's when we realized: He was bolted to the tree.

Matthew Fluke **Eureka, Calif.**

Now she's known as Dust Bunny

Our close friend Bunny was an avid cruiser, and she always wrote us about the funny things that happened to her—we called them "Bunny stories." Before she passed away, she asked us to scatter her ashes between Tahiti and Bora-Bora. Four of us sailed on the *Tahitian Princess* a year after her death. The bag of ashes had a hole, however, and when we removed it from its container, a good part of our friend fell on the floor. We grabbed a vacuum from the hall, removed her from the carpet, and had a ceremony with the rest of the ashes. To acknowledge the remainder of our dear friend, we put a lei on the vacuum and talked to "her" each day. She so would have loved her final Bunny story.

Candice J. Bischoff Warren, Mich.

The horse sure knew

While petting and admiring the Clydesdales at SeaWorld in Orlando, we decided to have a photo shoot. As the photographer was getting ready, she told my youngest son to reach back and pet the horse. We didn't realize until we got the photo exactly where he was touching.

Penny Valle Canton, Ga.

Pull that trick in America and you'll end up in Guantánamo

At the London Eye, policemen and Russian sailors were everywhere because Russian president Vladimir Putin was in town. The next day, at the Tower of London, it wasn't sailors who complicated our visit, it was Putin himself. Everywhere we went, he complicated our visit! On our way to the Greenwich observatory, we took a break in a park and accidentally left a duffel bag containing my jacket. Thirty minutes later, we realized our mistake and headed back. The park had been roped off. A policeman explained that President Putin would be arriving. "But my jacket!" I pleaded. "It's in the park!" The guard said it'd be a while before I could get it, and, to make matters worse, Putin was delayed. A strange package had been found in the park. "It's my jacket! It's in a little gray bag on a bench!" The policeman rolled his eyes and called in the news. I was led over to the bench, and, with the policeman standing at a safe distance, I opened the bag. Sure enough, my jacket was inside. This time we complicated Putin's visit!

Susan Sieveke **Yorba Linda, Calif.**

Pride goeth before a fall

My tour group gathered at the entrance of the Sistine Chapel in Vatican City. Among other instructions, our guide repeated several times in heavily accented English, "When entering you must look down—*very* important." The lady in front of me said, "I'm Baptist, not Catholic. They can't make me bow my head when I enter." Instead, she looked up at the ceiling, and then in a few seconds tripped down the three steps in front of *The Last Judgment*.

B. J. Clement **Reno, Nev.**

Sometimes the solution is right under your . . .

We bought a bottle of white wine to take back to our room at a small hotel in Sorrento, Italy. Since the wine wasn't chilled, I wandered down to the lobby bar and in the most minimal Italian tried to ask for ice and a receptacle to put it in. I was given a glass with 10 very small cubes. I scoured the room for a makeshift ice bucket. The bathroom sink was too small to accommodate the bottle, but the immaculate bidet—filled with cold water and the ice cubes—worked just fine!

Sue Nelson Portland, Ore.

One for the mantel

It wasn't just the crabs in black bean sauce that made Chinatown in Portland, Ore., memorable. There was also this restaurant's sign. Between giggles, I took a picture of my husband, Sam, standing under it. Our daughters are too young to comprehend what we found so amusing. Whew!

Claudia Fenner **Dix Hills, N.Y.**

It's called deep denial

I was on a flight to visit family, with my 2-year-old toddler and 7-week-old baby. Our first flight was a puddle jumper filled with businesspeople that got us from our rural town to Denver. I was nursing as discreetly as possible while trying to hand a toy to my toddler. The baby somehow got dislodged from feeding, and a stream of milk shot out of my breast. Unfortunately, the milk sprayed my neighbor's neck and shoulder, staining his shirt collar and suit. He never said a word. He just wiped his neck off and kept reading his reports.

Jennifer Aguilar **Durango, Colo.**

D'oh!

My husband and I were strolling along Las Ramblas in Barcelona when we spotted a metal sculpture of Bart Simpson on his skateboard, flanked by two metallic cyclists. My husband snapped a picture of me beside a cyclist. As I stepped away, I noticed a copper coin next to an empty can on the pavement. Having never seen a euro, I picked it up. Suddenly onlookers were shouting in Spanish and the "metal" cyclists erupted from their bikes. It was our first experience with living sculptures.

Lois Newlove Bellevue, Wash.

Trump's next wife

I was on a trip to Angkor Wat in Cambodia, and kids tried to sell me everything from cold drinks to tablecloths. One little girl had the best sales pitch I've heard in a long time. I was touring one of the quieter temples; she followed me while playing the flute. After a few minutes she stopped playing and said, "Sir, sir. You buy flute, four for a dollar!" Having no need for any flutes, I said, "What the heck am I going to do with four flutes?" With a disappointed look, she went into deep thought, then replied, "Okay, sir. *Three* for a dollar!"

Ian Gough **Winter Park, Colo.**

Four whiskeys before lunch and we're "allergic," too

While touring Scotland, my husband suggested devoting a day to exploring the Spey Valley—more specifically, to visiting some of the distilleries. On our third or fourth stop that morning, we were graciously received by a friendly, knowledgeable host. After hearing my husband's request for a "wee dram" of the house specialty, the host turned to me. "And for you, ma'am?" he asked. It was clear that he found my polite refusal perplexing. "And ye've come all this way for naught, then?" I explained that I can't drink whiskey, or any other liquor, because I'm allergic to alcohol. He asked, in a genuinely concerned tone of voice, "My God, woman, can't they do something for you?"

Joan Brown **Billings, Mont.**

Welcome to veganism

"Eat it first and ask what it is later" was my mom's motto on our two trips to Japan. One night, I ordered grilled eel. The cook lifted my dinner out of a bucket of water and, with a thud, drove an ice pick through the eel's eye. I could have sworn the eel was still wiggling when he placed it over the coals. As I pointed at the grill, the cook's wife presented me with a small dish bearing a maroon morsel of meat garnished with a lettuce leaf. My sister and I were peering at it when suddenly it began to throb! I screamed. It was the still-beating heart of my eel.

Emily Mosqueda **Eugene, Ore.**

Love hurts

On a cruise from Tahiti, my wife and I opted for a snorkeling excursion. She kept insisting that I allow a man to dangle fish over me to feed the stingrays. I told her no several times before deciding that I should confront my fear. When I got next to the man with the fish, however, a stingray latched onto my nipple, creating an incredibly painful wound. The ship's doctor said he'd never heard of such an incident, adding that the underside of a female ray is white, and maybe when the male saw my belly, he tried to mate with me instead.

Richard A. Wood Las Vegas, Nev.

He was hoping for Splenda

My friend Peggy and I were watching television at the A'Zambezi River Lodge near Victoria Falls, Zimbabwe, when we heard a loud crash. Having climbed onto the balcony, a baboon was making his way through our door. Once inside, he went straight to the coffeepot, took some packets of sugar, and left. Lucky for us, I don't drink coffee and Peggy likes hers black.

Craig B. Draheim **Battle Creek, Mich.**

Fierce!

In southern Irian Jaya, an Indonesian province in New Guinea, my friend Valerie and I hired two Indonesians and their motorboat for a five-day trip through the land of the Asmats. We brought tobacco and salt for the chief, who let us stay overnight for a few rupiahs, or $2. In the morning we were met by several male villagers. One was in full warrior feathers, with a shell piece through his nose—and he was also wearing the bright-green sunglasses I'd given his son the night before.

Lynda Howland **Pittsford, N.Y.**

Holy cowabunga!

On the last leg of my journey to the Samye Monastery in Tibet, I climbed on the back of an old flatbed truck filled with about 25 Buddhist monks. The truck lurched to a start, and we all grabbed for the sides and the struts overhead to keep from toppling like tenpins. Suddenly, one of the monks stood up and began riding "no hands" while the rest of us hung on for dear life. In a wide-footed stance with knees bent, the young man extended his arms forward from under his billowy maroon robe, expertly shifting his weight as the truck jarred over ruts and around curves. "You should see this!" I called to the others in the back. "This dude is surfing!" The other monks smiled and nodded in agreement, appreciating the fact that the amazing skill of their brother had not gone unnoticed by a foreigner.

Wayne Jeronimus Calistoga, Calif.

Hell is a tourist trap

In Rothenburg, Germany, my friend and I took the Night Watchman's Tour. When we asked the guide if he could recommend a restaurant, he said, "Go to hell." After seeing the shocked expression on our faces, he said he'd explain during the tour. Sure enough, we eventually came to a restaurant called Zur Höll—or "To Hell."

Angela Migliore **Framingham, Mass.**

Look what happened to the last trespassers

My sister and I were at the sculpture museum in Middelheim Park, in Antwerp, Belgium, when I commented that all the sculptures had the same title and artist—after all, the text was identical from statue to statue. My sister kindly translated it for me: DO NOT WALK ON THE GRASS.

Phyllis Walker Pinecrest, Fla.

Todos menos tú

Hoping to learn Spanish, I arranged to stay in the sleepy beach community of Dominical, Costa Rica, for an immersion program. The older couple I was staying with didn't speak English, so when I desperately needed a shower after arriving, I asked my host father for a towel in the best Spanish I could muster. My question appeared to embarrass him. I kept trying, and he went to consult his wife— who came back with a maxi pad. After exchanging many gestures, we eventually resolved the matter. Who knew *toalla* was slang for "maxi pad"?

Rebecca Gates **San Francisco, Calif.**

You are what you . . . tweet!

We did our own cooking when renting a house on Mexico's Soliman Bay. At the produce stand, there were several varieties of grains and nuts. One of the grains looked familiar, close to brown rice, and the vegetarian among us approved the choice. We cooked it for over an hour, but it still tasted oaky, so we cooked it longer and added seasoning. The property manager and the caretaker stopped in as we were about to eat. They were in awe of our ignorance. We had cooked a bag of birdseed.

Brenda Bluske El Verano, Calif.

Worst banana ever

Excited to stretch my legs during a drive in South Africa's Kruger National Park, I hopped out of the SUV, took a deep breath, and turned around to see a vervet monkey ransacking my bag. I chased it away, only to realize that it had scampered off with one of my precious few tampons. The monkey peeled it open, trying to figure out how to eat it while fighting off robbery attempts by the other monkeys. All I could do was sputter indignantly, "That @#$% monkey stole my tampon!"

Diane Fleeks Fairbanks, Alaska

"Easy-egress" is more like it

Moms and grandmas on our Interhostel tour of China were intrigued with the easy-access pants worn by diaperless toddlers. It became our mission to photograph a youngster wearing them, but this proved difficult: As soon as parents would see us eyeing their little one, they'd whisk the child around, assuming we wanted to capture the baby's face. After one Beijing dad presented me with several front-view photo ops, I waited until his attention was elsewhere, then snuck up from behind.

Nancy Shephard Stockton, Calif.

Some women just won't take a hint

When my wife and I went to Thailand for our 10th wedding anniversary, it took a lot of persuading to convince her to leave our 9-year-old son with his grandparents. Naturally, we missed our son, so toward the end, we decided to make a "treasure box" for him, filled with trinkets from the trip. At a 7-Eleven, I showed what I thought were Yu-Gi-Oh! cards to my wife (our son is obsessed with them). She burst out laughing and said, "I don't think our son is old enough for condoms."

Byron Lee Portola Valley, Calif.

Page 192 will give 'em even more of a shock

Upon arrival at our hotel in Nice, France, after a long day of travel, I told our daughters to wash their hands before dinner. They had been in the bathroom for five minutes when I asked what was taking so long. "Mom, we washed up so well in the baby sink!" they said with pride. I explained that the "baby sink" was actually a bidet, upon which they asked the inevitable question: "What's a bidet?"

Christina McGraw **Sammamish, Wash.**

Shaggy goes to China

My friend and I rented bikes and cycled out to the village of Baisha, outside of Lijiang, China. As we were exploring the town, a friendly woman invited us to her home. We walked to her house, where we enjoyed tea and peanuts. Then she pulled out a box of traditional dresses and cheerily motioned for me to try one on. After dressing us up, she paraded us around her courtyard, taking pictures with our cameras. We gradually realized that she expected a modest tip, which we were more than glad to give for such a bizarre experience.

Rich Fowler San Francisco, Calif.

First they suck your dignity

Traversing the Irish countryside, my friends and I came across many great photo ops, including a large mosquito sculpture on the front lawn of a quaint cottage. I was posing with the menacing insect when I looked over to find several people peering out the window, photographing what they must've thought was a *very* strange American.

Casey O'Connell **Pensacola, Fla.**

Maybe you were swearing in sign language

Since I don't speak Turkish or French, I used hand gestures to select from an array of spa treatments at the Hammam de la Mosquée de Paris, a Turkish bath in one of Europe's largest mosques. I wasn't sure exactly what I ordered, but I understood that a refreshment of sweet Turkish tea and crushed dates would be included. I was handed a small bowl filled with what I figured were the crushed dates, and I set out to enjoy steaming buckets of water poured onto marble lounging platforms, a steam room, and a marble hot tub. Finally, while munching on my sweets, I wandered into the back room, where a woman was to give me a loofah scrub before my massage. I was embarrassed to learn that I had been eating the soap.

Paula Nailon Tucson, Ariz.

Monkey story number one

My boyfriend and I were in Costa Rica on a boat ride in the Damas Estuary when our guide pulled ashore, stood up, and started grunting. Monkeys came out of the trees and onto the boat. To my boyfriend's surprise, one gave him a nice, warm welcome by peeing down his back.

Patricia Daniel **Austin, Tex.**

Monkey story number two

At the Hotel Costa Verde in Quepos, Costa Rica, I put some banana on top of a light, hoping the scent would entice the monkeys out of the trees. It worked: They arrived at the same time as a Japanese tour group. The monkeys pooped all over my white outfit, but I didn't care because I had so much fun feeding them—while the tour group took pictures, thinking it was a show!

Mollie Hejl **Spring, Tex.**

Bosom buggies

Because our rented VW Bug had no A/C, my wife and I were wearing our bathing suits as we drove through Baja California, and of course the windows were open. As we motored north at 60 mph, a wasp flew inside the car and into my wife's cleavage. She immediately started writhing and screaming. I stopped, pulled her from the car, and yanked her swimsuit down to her waist so the wasp could escape. In my haste to relieve her pain, I hadn't noticed a rather shocked Mexican family having lunch in their yard. (Our son, Matt, later drew this illustration to commemorate the moment.)

Gary MacFarland **Snohomish, Wash.**

Paging Quentin Tarantino . . .

I felt a tug on my bag while walking in Barcelona. As I spun around, a man ripped the bag off and ran down an alley. My rage turned into adrenaline. "I don't think so, you #$%&@¢!" I yelled, sprinting. I was ready to tackle him when I found myself skidding across the dirty pavement—the guy must have had an accomplice, because somebody tripped me. I sprang back up with bloody knees and wrists and limped down the street. A bartender locking up saw the thief coming toward him. He grabbed hold of the thief's collar, raised him off the ground, and tossed him through a window. He then threw the thief into the street and proceeded to rifle through his pockets. I grabbed my bag out of a puddle and stared at the bartender, unable to comprehend what had happened. The bartender pocketed the thief's ID and offered me the wallet. I pulled out €5, and threw the thief's wallet back in the street. Then I kicked the thief in the leg and treated the bartender to a nightcap.

Kate Snow **Minneapolis, Minn.**

Coming soon to late-night cable: *Brokestrap Mountain*

It was hot in Puerto Vallarta, so I wore my bathing suit on a horseback ride. After two hours, my horse started galloping home. As an amateur rider, I did my best to control him—but I had less success with the straps on my bathing suit. Down went the right one and then the left. I couldn't do anything to fix it—my hands were busy holding the reins! Cars paused and people craned their necks as I flew by. It wasn't until we reached the stables that I was able to regain composure and put my top back on.

Marcia Johns **Sandy, Utah**

You just ordered a new suit

At six foot four and 380 pounds, I got used to standing out while in Chongqing, China. People stared, some folks patted my stomach, and a few even walked into street poles while looking me over. One shopkeeper took it a step further. He ran out of his store and motioned for me to stand still, then hurried back inside. He emerged with a tape measure and proceeded to measure my height and girth, each time holding it up to the small crowd that had gathered. I knew enough of the culture not to take offense—I was being paid an honor.

Clarence Holbrook **Loveland, Colo.**

So not a kangaroo

I was enjoying the beautiful scenery on a bus tour in southwest Washington State when, in a meadow, I saw a wild animal with its ears perked up. "Look, look!" I yelled excitedly. "A kangaroo!" The man sitting behind me peered from his window. "Lady, we're not in Australia," he said. "And that's not a kangaroo, it's a deer taking a crap."

Virginia Andersen Tumwater, Wash.

Knowing it is half the battle

A few years ago, my friend Bill and I traveled to St. John, in the U.S. Virgin Islands, for my brother's wedding. One day we were given access to a car to tour the island. We soon came across a junction in the road where there were more choices than were indicated on our map. Using my best instincts, I picked a route. We drove for a short while and realized that I had probably made the wrong choice. Then we came upon a sign that proved it.

Anna Slamka New York, N.Y.

Separated at birth?

While trekking the Annapurna circuit in Nepal, I stopped for a chai on the way to Thorung Phedi base camp and saw a goat in the tea-hut window. I asked a guide if I could take his photo alongside the animal, and he was more than happy to oblige. Apparently, the goat was pretty happy, too.

Marc Weisman Patchogue, N.Y.

Free with every issue of
Plumber's Monthly

After finishing college in London, I flew to Spain and set off alone from Barcelona on a two-month Eurail pass. Eager to meet other young travelers, I boarded a train with the intent of finding interesting company. The conductor, who didn't like the idea of a woman traveling alone, insisted that I sit with a Spanish family. Not 15 minutes into our trip, an attractive but seedy-looking man smiled through the cabin's glass door. He opened the door and tried to speak to me in Spanish. I shook my head to indicate that I didn't understand, so he switched to French. Thrilled to find a language that I understood, he jabbered at me, much to the annoyance of the family. Harsh words were exchanged, but the suitor continued flirting. When he entered the cabin, it was too much for the nearly toothless grandmother, who rose from her seat and beat the man with a rolled-up magazine until he left. When she sat down, her magazine unrolled to reveal a foot-long, three-quarter-inch-thick metal pipe.

Jocelyn Canfield Kelemen **Abingdon, Pa.**

So you turned around and walked out . . . right?

My sister and I figured we'd find a B&B while in Frankfurt, Germany—what we hadn't counted on was the huge international convention that had every room booked. We scoured the city looking for a place to spend the night. Around midnight, in a rather crummy part of town, we grabbed the first motel room we could get. The clerk asked how long we planned to stay. "Only one night," we answered. He looked at us strangely, and asked, "The whole night?" We had stumbled into the red-light district, where the rooms rent by the hour.

Ginny Cheek **Friendswood, Tex.**

That's a new one

My husband and I took a cruise to Tahiti, and while on a side trip to Mooréa we went snorkeling with stingrays. When I felt something stroke my bottom, I figured it was just someone's fin. After a couple of seconds I felt it again—a definite stroke. I stood up, and a man popped up and looked at me with a shocked expression. "I thought you were a stingray," he gasped, "and I was trying to pet you!"

Sue Oberholtzer **Cambria, Calif.**

Purple rain,
purple raaaaaaiiin

Holi is an Indian festival of colors that celebrates good over evil. My friends began by dropping six buckets of pink dye on me from the roof of my guesthouse. Next we ran to the biggest city square in Jaisalmer, greeting others with smears of color. Large groups of boys began to march with arsenals of dye-filled squirt guns, powder, and drums. Colored water squished in my shoes and powder gathered in my eyes, ears, and mouth. Later that day I shampooed four times and scrubbed my skin raw but still ended up looking like Barney, the purple dinosaur, for two weeks.

Alexis Hoffmann Kalamazoo, Mich.

Next thing you know, the wise men are packing their bags

As I was checking in to a B&B in London, the innkeeper asked if I wanted to be knocked up in the morning. I was absolutely speechless, but the couple behind me saw my consternation and whispered, "Say yes." Reluctantly, I did. The next morning I heard a knock at my door. "Who is it?" I asked. A male voice from the hall replied, "Just knocking up to let you know that breakfast will be ready in 20 minutes, miss."

Nancy Hesler **W. Chicago, Ill.**

They call her Lady Luck . . .

On a recent cruise, I sat down at a bingo table. A woman wearing a vest with a ton of name badges on it asked if the adjacent seat was open. Mama Lou, it turns out, cruises 75 percent of the year, and the badges are gifts from the cruise line's employees. I offered to buy her a game card. "Oh, I don't play anymore, honey," she replied. "I just bring good luck to whoever I sit next to!" I'd never come close to winning bingo in my life. The bingo began, and she giggled like a young girl as I won three of the next four bingo games.

Steve Mullen Chesterfield, Mo.

You'll thrive in corporate culture

My friend Ellen and I, while at the Daintree Rainforest in Australia, spent the day with a guide who took us hiking through areas with various animals and plants. One of the most bizarre experiences was when we were asked to lick the backside of a green tree ant. Yes, its butt. We both laughed and said, "You've got to be kidding." The guide held the ant in his fingers—it was so small you could hardly see it. We took our turns licking away. Never in my wildest dreams did I imagine I would lick the backside of an ant, think it would taste good—just like lemon-lime soda!—and live to tell about it.

Laurie Bushkoff **Silver Spring, Md.**

That's a loaded question

I knew I'd look out of place in Japan, as I'm more than six feet tall and have a huge Afro. Nonetheless, I chose to study abroad there for a semester. I joined the Shiga University Basketball Club, where I met a great group of guys, and on my final night, we went to a bar called Sugimoto's. Wednesday was *gaijin* (foreigner) night, so I blew out my hair. One of the Japanese regulars took a long look at my hair, and finally got the courage to ask, "If you are curly up there, are you straight down there?" I had no idea how to respond.

Zachary Colman **West Bloomfield, Mich.**

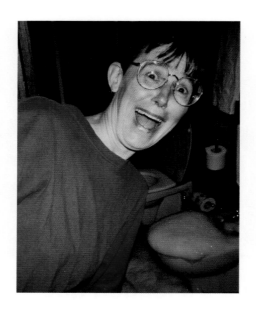

If you were a bidet, you'd be angry, too

As we settled into our Florence hotel, we discovered an out-of-control bidet frothing all over. I found a maid, whose eyes got big when she saw the mess. She yelled down the hall, and another maid came in. They exchanged a few words, glanced at me, and burst into laughter. We'll never know what they said, but I suspect it was something like "Was she trying to shampoo her hair in the bidet?"

Maryka Biaggio Portland, Ore.

Laugh hard enough at yourself and it'll block out the sound of everyone else laughing at you

I was amazed at the number of doctors' offices on every street in Switzerland, and when I began to feel ill, I was relieved that it'd be easy to find help. I walked into what I assumed to be a clinic and announced to the receptionist and a roomful of people that I had a bladder infection and needed antibiotics—only to discover that I was in an insurance office! What I had taken for Red Cross signs were just red-and-white Swiss flags.

Pamela Long **Wentzville, Mo.**

Kids smear the darnedest things

I was on the beach in Pochomil, Nicaragua, when a friend brought out a cake covered with frosting flowers—my niece had told her it was my birthday. Several kids immediately flocked around us. After I served the cake, all that was left was frosting. When two boys asked if they could have it, I said yes. Little did I know they'd have as much fun painting their faces with the frosting as eating it!

Elizabeth Vollrath Stevens Point, Wis.

Italian guys can get away with anything

Waiting for my return flight from Rome, I fell into conversation with an Italian gentleman. I raved on about all the hiking I'd gotten to do in Abruzzi, and added that although I thought Rome was beautiful and exciting, I'd been somewhat disappointed that no one had pinched my derriere. We both laughed as he assured me that Italian men were sensitive to the same women's-lib issues as American men. We discussed Italian literature and art until I had to board my plane to Boston. He walked me to the gate, and as I passed through the checkpoint, I felt an enthusiastic pinch on my buttocks. I spun around to discover the "gentleman" grinning and winking. "Now your trip is complete," he said.

Holly Carroll Arlington, Mass.

Don't point it at us

In Kerala, India, I was on a gorgeous drive through the tea plantations when, on my way up the side of a mountain, I saw a beautifully decorated truck on the side of the road and pulled over to photograph it. I had just snapped the photo when, to my shock and disbelief, the truck slowly began to keel over and roll down the hill into the tea plantation. Who knew the camera shutter would be too loud?

Peter Richmond **Saratoga, Calif.**

Like your husband isn't an animal

My mother, my husband, and I noticed that most Chinese people dress formally in China. In fact, it wasn't uncommon to see Chinese tourists in suits and ties. When we got to Guilin, the weather was unseasonably warm, and my husband wore shorts. A Chinese girl soon wrapped herself around my husband's leg. She was fascinated with his hairy legs, petting his knee like he was an animal.

Delia Rhodes **Jamestown, N.C.**

Quickly followed by "My deductible!"

Neither my husband, Dale, nor I gave a thought to his motion sickness before boarding a sunset cruise in Hawaii. When the skipper realized my husband's plight, he said, "Move to the back rail, don't throw up into the wind, and here's a cup of water to rinse your mouth." A woman with the same trouble soon joined us. Suddenly, she tossed the water overboard and upchucked into her cup. One of the crew, fearing that this was grossing out the other passengers, grabbed the cup and threw it overboard. "My teeth!" she yelled.

Kitty Ruosch Holmen, Wis.

Indian giver!

Some friends and I stayed in a small village in India where many of the locals had never seen foreigners. One man was so excited he gave me a baby goat. I smiled for a minute before trying to hand it back. The man firmly insisted I keep the goat. Since no one spoke English, I couldn't explain why it was impossible for me to keep it. The other villagers began to crowd around us, so I accepted his gift. The goat was mine for the rest of my stay, and seeing no other option, I ended up re-gifting it to another family a few nights later.

Jenny Otvos **Raleigh, N.C.**

More Disney Imagineering

My husband and I, checking out the various hotels on our last trip to Walt Disney World Resort in Florida, were amazed by the Animal Kingdom Lodge with its wildlife visible from the verandas off the main lobby. As we walked from one overlook to another, we saw a sign describing the blue crane. It was certainly an interesting species.

Jan Capasso **Murrysville, Pa.**

Open mouth, insert . . . foot

It had been a long and exhausting day at Epcot, and my husband and I were on the bus back to our hotel. Nearby, a young woman was holding a baby—the child was completely relaxed, arms and legs splayed. Smiling at the woman, my husband nodded at the child, and said, "I wish I could do that." There was an awkward silence, during which we realized that the mother was discreetly nursing. She burst out laughing, and we exited at the next stop—even though it wasn't ours.

Sara Thompson **Statesville, N.C.**

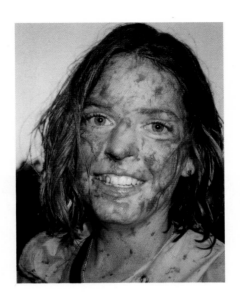

"But next time, use Jell-O!"

My friend and I were walking through Bhaktapur, Nepal, when an innocent puddle fight progressed into an out-of-control mud war. By the time we had wrestled each other to the ground, we realized that the sight of a man and a woman mud wrestling might be offensive to the Nepalese. Indeed, a crowd had gathered. We slowly stood up. An old man stepped forward. We expected the worst— until he threw open his arms and proclaimed, "You have given Bhaktapur many good memories!"

Monica McKay Cincinnati, Ohio

We can hear it now: "Draw at ten paces"

I was standing by the Hermitage in St. Petersburg, Russia, trying to stay warm, when I noticed a man with a sketch pad staring in my direction. He was drawing me, so I took out my sketchbook and started to draw him. People gathered around him, and it soon became apparent that he was the true artist. We shared a few laughs and our drawings, and I left and went on my way.

Adam Tennen Scottsdale, Ariz.

Land

(Slow dumb runners, grains and vegetables)

d Lamb Shank, Wok Tossed Greens, Cocoa Bean Ragout
t Mignon with Mashed Potatoes and Red Wine Sauce $1?
getarian Mezze Platter for Vegans and Tree Huggers $10

Side Dishes

We tell you that 'You are beautiful' All Night Long $2.00
Garden Greens Tossed in our House Vinaigrette $4.00
Wok Tossed Vegetables $4.00
Macaroni and Cheese $5.00

Restaurant Bobby Chinn Rules:

Picky, picky

At Restaurant Bobby Chinn in Hanoi, Vietnam, my wife secretly ordered me a side dish called "We tell you that 'You are beautiful' All Night Long." (It was listed on the menu for $2.) When the waiter brought our food, he looked me in the eye and, much to my surprise, told me that I was beautiful. This continued for the entire meal. Between the waiter, the bartender, and the busboy, I was told 10 times that I was beautiful. The food and service were hands down the best we had in Vietnam. My only complaint: I wish that we'd had a waitress!

Jason Mullin Singapore

Tanzanian humor

My husband, my children, and I were dismayed to find that none of our checked luggage had arrived with us at Kilimanjaro airport in Tanzania, and wouldn't for three days. The next morning, our guide took us into town. I'm plus-size, and I didn't see any clothes that would fit me. I asked the proprietor of a shop if he had anything that might work. "Not in this country," he replied. "Try Kenya."

Susan G. Buchanan **Baltimore, Md.**

Isn't it nice that they take her everywhere they go?

For our belated honeymoon, my husband and I took a 15,000-mile cross-country trip through the United States and Canada. On Interstate 40, on the way to Albuquerque, we spotted this vehicle. We knew there had to be more to the story, but I'm afraid we didn't get a chance to meet up with the driver to find out what it might be.

Nicole O'Shea-Holohan Mill Neck, N.Y.

Me-*ow*!

My husband and I were honeymooning in Jamaica, and on our way back from the beach, we passed some stepping stones, so we ventured to see where they led. We came upon cages of exotic animals and various secluded areas with hammocks. Since we were hidden from view, I tried an exotic move: Purring and growling at my husband, I made a panther-like crawl onto a hammock. The hammock went into a spin and flipped me while I screamed and tried to hold on. My husband began snapping pictures. After he untangled me, I made him baby me for the rest of the day.

Tammy Smith Caledonia, Miss.

Say it loud, say it proud

In Zanzibar, my husband and I took a spice-farm
tour with our Australian travel mate, Mac. The locals
had been pointing and laughing at him all day,
so finally he asked a worker what was so funny.
"Your shirt!" she said. Mac had ruined a shirt while
on safari, so he'd bought a new one at the market.
The Swahili word on the shirt, MZUNGU, loosely
translates as "white boy tourist."

Denise Jones Issaquah, Wash.

If you can't join 'em, lick 'em

My wife, our two sons, and I were visiting Mont Tremblant, northwest of Montreal, and decided to take a day trip to Oméga animal park. We arrived, bought carrots, and drove slowly down the road. Almost immediately we were surrounded by a mass of moose. With camera in hand, I went to lower my window for an unobstructed view, but in my zeal I lowered all four windows at once, and my family began to scream. If you've never had a moose shove his head into your car and lick your face— each drooling slurp going from chin to forehead— you can't imagine what my 6-year-old, Ethan, was going through. He was strapped in his car seat, and his head was bouncing like a bobble-head doll's. I couldn't roll up the window and I couldn't drive ahead. Only a well-aimed carrot pitched past the moose's head by my older son, Julian, diverted its attention long enough for us to escape.

Paul Kramer Upper Montclair, N.J.

It helps if you're wearing a habit

On a solo trip to Ireland, I got stranded in a town outside Waterford. There were no trains, taxis, or buses, and every shop, restaurant, and B&B was closed. Pondering my predicament, I walked awhile, then rested on a stone wall in front of a large, old house. Eventually several nuns strolled by and suggested I hitch a ride to Rosslare. But car after car passed me by. Finally a truck driver hesitated, then told me to get in. "Long time getting a lift?" he asked. I nodded. "You were standing with your baggage in front of the insane asylum."

Polly Mason **Borrego Springs, Calif.**

It was proof that they like to live on the edge

My boyfriend not only talks to strangers when he travels, but also adopts their heavily accented English. In Egypt, Patrick asked our cabbie, "So, you good driver?" The driver crossed three lanes of traffic, slammed on the brakes, and parked on the highway. I worried that he had taken offense. He got out of the car and opened the trunk. After a short while—with my imagination running wild— he came back brandishing an issue of *National Geographic*. An article described him as the cabbie the magazine's photographers use when in Egypt—proof that he was in fact a good driver.

Monica Redmond La Crosse, Wis.

Let's hope he didn't find out the squishy way

While my husband and I were visiting Inle Lake in Myanmar, our guide took us to the Nga Phe Kyaung Monastery, known for its trained jumping cats. As custom requires, we removed our shoes before entering. We watched a few minutes, smiled at the odd spectacle, and made a small donation. We were less amused, however, when we discovered that the cats had made a donation of their own—in my husband's shoes!

Lori MacDonald Fairfax, Va.

Wait until he learns about those tiny cigarettes

A longtime friend invited us to attend her wedding in Cancún. The day after the ceremony, a group of us with kids in tow hired a driver to shuttle us to various sites. We spent the day traveling to ruins, parks, and beaches, quenching our thirst with beer and tequila. As the day drew to a close, we ate at a quaint cantina, with more beer and tequila. There was no doubt that hiring a designated driver was the right thing to do. The next day, my 7-year-old son came to me with a question: "Mom, what was the matter with Karen yesterday? She was acting kind of funny." I was pretty sure I knew where this was headed, but I did my best to explain that maybe she had had a little too much to drink. "I don't think so," he replied. "She was only drinking from those tiny glasses."

Debbie Thomas Fort Lauderdale, Fla.

Hair today, gone tomorrow

On a four-week bike tour from San Diego to Cabo
San Lucas, my boyfriend and I always got a warm
welcome from the locals. In La Paz, we met a
barber and avid cyclist who invited us to spend the
night; he wouldn't take no for an answer. His wife,
however, was tired of stinky cyclists in her house
and politely said, "Absolutely not." So instead of
the guest bedroom, we slept on the floor of the
barber's shop. We loved it! It was clean, and the
barber visited with us late into the night as we
shared cycling stories and practiced our Spanish.

Jessica Drollette Bend, Ore.

Safe phone sex: The new frontier in public health

While in a Peruvian village, my friend Gladys needed to use the bathroom—basically a hole in the ground surrounded by a fence. Only later did she realize that she was missing her cell phone. We ran back to the latrine and fished around with two sticks. The phone looked and smelled as bad as we thought it would, so we submerged it in two pails of water and gave it a Clorox bath, then wrapped it in a plastic bag to dry. Suddenly, the phone rang! Gladys answered it, using the bag as a mitt. It was her husband calling, and through gales of laughter we told him our story—although all he could really hear was a crinkling bag.

Bonnie Laycock Wichita, Kans.

You know the old saying: Red thighs at night, sailor's delight

My husband and I were enjoying an alfresco dinner in Nassau, Bahamas, when I asked one of the other patrons to snap a photo with the sunset behind us. The picture came out fantastic, although on closer inspection I noticed that my bright red underwear was peeking through! I suppose I would've been better off wearing undies that matched my dress. . . .

Caroline Tetschner Mundelein, Ill.

Just checking the weather . . .

I was in a kangaroo sanctuary in Australia with friends when I caught sight of this kangaroo. The kids started asking what the protrusion was, and I wondered how to explain it to them. But as we got closer, we realized that it was a joey's foot sticking out from its mother's pouch. Whew!

Tina Dannemiller Pensacola, Fla.

And we thought Wiglet was one of Pooh's friends

My husband and I were horseback riding near the California redwoods. I finally got my horse to gallop, but she wouldn't stop. I was passing other riders, ducking under low-hanging tree limbs—or so I thought. I went to straighten my hair, and to my horror, it was gone! I looked over my shoulder and, sure enough, there hung my clip-on ponytail wiglet.

Barbara White Surprise, Ariz.

We see one big clue that he was happy to see you

My husband, Keith, and I were touring Indonesia when we visited the province of Irian Jaya. We went to the Baliem Valley, where the Dani people have maintained their way of life for centuries. Unknown to us, our guide had arranged a special welcome. As our van pulled into the entrance of the remote lodging, about 40 native men armed with spears, bows, and arrows rushed from the bushes. Their wardrobe consisted mostly of feather headdresses and penis sheaths made from gourds held in place by cords around their waists. Needless to say, we were scared to death. Finally we realized that it was all an act, and they gave us a friendly welcome. But have you ever shaken hands with a man wearing only a gourd?

Joyce Brooks Evant, Tex.

You and us both

My husband and I were at a restaurant in Cap Haitien, Haiti, when I ordered consommé. I was expecting a clear broth, but in Haitian cuisine, however, consommé means stew. No problem. At the time, food was scarce, and folks made do with what they had. There were bits of vegetables, cassava dumplings, and goat—the available meat at that moment. Goat is naturally bony, so I wasn't shocked to be sucking on a lot of bones. What I didn't expect to suck on was a row of teeth!

Cathy Buttazoni Edmonton, Alb.

His left hand, however . . .

My girlfriend and I got lost while hiking on Mexico's Baja peninsula. *Christ!* I said to myself. *Where's the car?* Reaching the top of the hill, we were amazed to behold a sight that made my earlier exclamation eerily prophetic—a giant statue of Jesus. And his right hand was pointing directly to our car.

Gene Pembroke Lester, Pa.

When he puts his bifocals on, somebody's gonna pay

My husband, Donald, and I were celebrating his retirement with a trip to Alaska. We stopped just outside Fairbanks to look at a portion of the Alaska pipeline, when I spotted the perfect photo op. What better way to memorialize the event?

Georgia Reilly Vienna, Va.

We'll assume you explained it to her

Thirty years after my husband and I were married on Mount Tantalus, Oahu, he surprised me with a trip to Maui to celebrate our anniversary. We took three connecting flights, and we received snacks on each flight. I saved all of the packages in a clean airsickness bag, and on the last leg, when the flight attendant saw me holding the closed bag, she offered to take it from me. "No, thanks," I replied. "I'm going to eat it later." Her eyes widened, and she cautiously moved away.

Lorna Fleming Munroe Falls, Ohio

Cutting to the chase

While studying abroad in Beijing, I visited the Great Wall—but in a strange twist, I became the tourist attraction. The locals marveled at my long blond hair and asked me to pose for countless photos. One vendor approached me and commented on my "golden" hair. I smiled and nodded. "Golden hair," she said. "I buy." I gave her a strange look and declined. She started offering me money. Not wanting to give up my hair, I kept refusing. She got agitated and walked away. I was heading back to the bus when she came chasing after me with a pair of scissors and yelling, "Golden hair! Golden hair!" I ran faster than I had in a *long* time.

Nicole Andersen Santa Barbara, Calif.

Someone has a bright future as an acupuncturist

While in Ecuador's Amazon region, I got to spend a night in the hut of an indigenous family. Since I don't speak Quechua, I brought a variety of games I could explain simply by demonstrating them. I was delighted to hear the enthusiastic chatter and laughter of the kids in the other room after I showed them how to play pick-up sticks. Imagine my surprise when the youngest child came out to show me her version of the game.

Karen Bennett Thornton, Colo.

Busted!

My husband and I were staying in a waterfront bungalow on Bora-Bora when I spotted two rays swimming toward us. I ran to the deck where my husband was sitting and yelled, "Look at those!" He immediately came inside. The woman who was sunbathing topless on the deck next door also hightailed it into her bungalow. I guess they both misunderstood what I was referring to.

Shelly Galloway St. George Island, Fla.

Gimme five, bro

Deep in the Peruvian jungle, I met a girl who had no friends her age, so her parents had given her a baby howler monkey. When I held her for a picture, the monkey got jealous and slapped my eyeball!

James Hilpert **Santa Cruz, Calif.**

When they say U-Haul . . .

In the Angkor area of Cambodia, our bus had to stop for a large obstruction—a house in the road. Most of the houses are built on stilts, which makes it easy for people to walk under them. This house was being moved by about 50 people, who lifted it and carried it 5 to 10 feet at a time. We got out to take pictures. The movers noticed us, and after a move, they'd turn around, wave, and flex their muscles.

Rob Taylor Edgewater, Md.

Third-World McNuggets

I was a Peace Corps volunteer in Sierra Leone, and when I came across a familar meat—such as chicken—I jumped at the opportunity to eat it. Once, when making the long trip to the capital city, I stopped at a roadside restaurant where a woman sold barbecued chicken. I bypassed legs and thighs and selected a skewer of chicken pieces. The first bite crunched between my teeth, and then I felt a substance ooze onto my tongue. Only after taking the piece out of my mouth did I notice the eye sockets and beak. I gave the remainder of my chicken-head kebab to the delighted boy next to me and went back to purchase a drumstick.

Jim Laden Portland, Ore.

It certainly goes nicely with your red neck

When my friend Margie and I arrived at the isolated Vietnamese village of the Black Hmong people, word of our visit spread quickly. When we went to take a photo, preparations began immediately for a show of their best finery. Girls and grown women bustled about, giggling as they wrapped and secured layer after layer of intricate fabrics. The finishing touch was the application of a blackening root to their teeth, a cosmetic custom the women practiced every night from the age of 9—one that they urged me to try on at least one tooth.

Tamar Dolwig Aptos, Calif.

He's just bitter because he never evolved

I was at a raja's palace in India when my friend Howard suggested that I take a photograph of him with one of the many wild monkeys that roam freely on the palace's grounds. After handing me his camera, he inched closer to a monkey sitting calmly on a wall. I snapped the first picture, of the two peacefully making eye contact—and by sheer luck, I also captured the moment that followed. Fortunately, the monkey didn't pursue further.

Dean Divis Greenfield Center, N.Y.

Should've said baseball

My coworker Craig, who is six feet, 11 inches tall, got a lot of attention while we were traveling through China. He actually appeared to believe he was some sort of royalty. We were having fun with his celebrity status, allowing the locals to join us in pictures, until we ran into a middle-aged woman who was clearly unimpressed. In broken English, she asked Craig who he was and what he did for a living. He claimed to be a famous basketball player. She shook her head and waved him away. He asked why she didn't believe him. "You no basketball player," she said. "You fat like Buddha."

Susan Waters Milan, Mich.

This little piggy went to the bar

I recently went to a sailing school in St. Croix, in the U.S. Virgin Islands, with my husband and a friend. One day we went to visit the beer-drinking pigs that we'd seen advertised. We found the bar, but a sign said the pigs were refusing to drink the beer. I persuaded the owners to let me try. I leaned over the pigpen and opened the beer—and a pig got up and grabbed the can out of my hand! It gulped the beer down in a few seconds. I'm not sure who was more entertained, the pig or me!

Shirley Weidenhamer Venice, Fla.

We'd rather eat the stick

My husband and I try to fit in by eating the local delicacies. We ate ant eggs in Mexico and llama and guinea pig in Peru, but while in Hong Kong we finally put a stop to the tradition. Walking toward the Temple Street night market, we found a store that sold sun-dried foods such as mushrooms and shark fins, but what really caught our eye was one local dish we'd never try—lizard on a stick.

Macarena Scalia **South Miami, Fla.**

Five-second rule!

It was brutally hot in New Delhi, and my wife and I couldn't help noticing how everyone was enjoying iced fruit drinks. Even though we knew the ice was suspect, we broke down and ordered a mango drink. We started drinking on the spot. Suddenly, there was a commotion a few stalls away—a boy screaming at a cow. He bent down and picked up his bike, which the cow had knocked over. He knelt down and grabbed a block of ice from a pile of fresh cow manure. He wiped it off, strapped it to his bike, and took it to our vendor.

Alfie Blanch Pasadena, Calif.

Black suits you

While on a Celebrity cruise, five of my senior-aged friends and I noted that our waiter was spending more time with an attractive 20-something lady and her mother than the six of us, so I chided him good-naturedly. He said if I came to dinner dressed like the young lady—attractively, in a black dress— I'd receive the same level of service. The next stop was Costa Rica, and I immediately went into town to secure a dress that I wore the next night. From that point on, service improved dramatically.

Don Laird Indialantic, Fla.

"Then slap knee"

I'd been told that the Japanese are unfailingly polite, and on a business trip to Osaka, I found it to be true. I was giving a lecture, and because Japanese audiences are traditionally quiet, I was trying a little tongue-in-cheek humor. They seemed to appreciate it. I asked the interpreter if they were understanding my humor. "Oh yes, Rick-san," she said. "I tell them, 'Is American joke. Please laugh.'"

Rick Tillman Tualatin, Ore.

Fast-forward instant replay!

While in Europe, my husband and I took photos everywhere. Then, at the Eiffel Tower, my husband screamed—he had accidentally reformatted the entire memory card. Our photos of Paris were gone. With a single day left, we decided to reshoot the photos we'd lost. We walked back through the Louvre, revisited the Champs-Elysées, and climbed the 774 steps up and down Notre Dame for a second time. We were even able to fit in a riverboat ride. In 14 hours we accomplished our mission, but friends back home are still wondering why we wore the same outfits our whole time in Paris.

Sabrina Kambayashi **Maineville, Ohio**

You'd prefer "chilly"?

I went to Bermuda with a few great friends who happen to be straitlaced, churchgoing women, and one day, we decided to rent mopeds. Guess what my nickname turned out to be.

Renae Kinsey Apollo Beach, Fla.

Telling you certainly defeats the purpose

While serving as a Peace Corps volunteer in Jolo, Philippines, I was invited to a banquet hosted by the community leader. The main course was a fruit salad served on a banana leaf. Thinking the leaf was part of the meal, I picked mine up and chewed on it. The others also chewed their leaves. After the meal, one of the braver guests told me that I'd eaten my plate—everyone else followed along simply so that I wouldn't be embarrassed by my actions.

Don Yates Normandy Beach, N.J.

Henny Youngman lives

While in Malta, I snapped a photograph of an old fisherman. Thinking it would be polite to start a conversation, I asked if he had a problem with his net. He stopped his mending. "I don't have a problem with my net," he said in perfect English. "I have a problem with my wife."

Doug Karlberg Bellingham, Wash.

He's just jealous of the guys over at Buckingham Palace

My husband and I were shopping in London's Knightsbridge district, and he was carrying some of our purchases. As we approached Harrods, we were somewhat intimidated by the building's Edwardian bulk. At the door stood a guard in full dress uniform. "May I bring the bag into your store?" asked my husband. "No, sir," the guard replied solemnly. "She'll have to wait outside."

Susan Douglass **Muncie, Ind.**

Xanax. Lithium. Maybe both

After getting an early-morning start en route to a fishing trip in northern Minnesota, I felt myself falling asleep at the wheel of my car. Seeing a wayside ahead, I realized that a 15-minute nap would rejuvenate me. I parked in front of a tree-lined area and dozed off. Unfortunately, while in my half-asleep state, I dreamed I was still driving—with my eyes closed. I snapped open my eyes, only to see a large pine tree dead ahead. Gripping the steering wheel and slamming down my foot on the lifeless brake pedal, I let out a bloodcurdling scream. A second later, I realized exactly what had happened. I started laughing wildly. This maniacal display didn't sit well with the couple parked next to me; they looked at each other, started their car, and made a hasty exit.

Chet Holmes Brookfield, Wis.

None of which explains why the feet get so much action

At Père Lachaise cemetery in Paris, my boyfriend and I were greeted by an unofficial guide who offered to show us Jim Morrison's grave. Along the way, we stopped at the tomb of Victor Noir. The guide said Noir had an erection for two days after dying, and that rubbing a certain area of the statue makes a woman fertile. I later learned that Noir was killed the day before his wedding and that a woman who kisses the statue's lips will find a husband by the year's end. The rubbing must work just as well, because my boyfriend had an engagement ring in his pocket and proposed a few hours later.

Vicky Shkreli Pacilli **Windsor, Ont.**

Warning: Lift that black sticker at your own risk

I was traveling around the Thai islands with my girlfriend when, on Ko Samui, she begged me to go on an elephant-riding tour. When she learned that the tour included a side trip to a monkey farm, my girlfriend was ecstatic—she's bananas about monkeys. I took a few shots of an unenthusiastic monkey on her shoulders, and then it was my turn. She and our guide burst out laughing: The monkey was pleasuring himself inches from my head.

Jesse Golland Isle of Palms, S.C.

Now explain the photo, son

When my friend and I stepped onto the dock at the port of Kuşadasi, Turkey, an older man approached us and offered a place to hang out, with promises of a Turkish barbecue. Since we were both starving, we decided to check it out. As we walked, the man tantalized us with talk of this magnificent barbecue, adding that there'd also be a belly dancer because it was "ladies' night." Excited for the show, we got a table and ate a fabulous dinner. Just as we finished our meals, the belly dancer finally appeared—and to our surprise, it was a man! Of course it was all in good fun, and we ended up having a great time.

Ryan Canter San Diego, Calif.

"Because you're the best thing since sliced bread"

In February, my husband took me to Isla Mujeres, Mexico, for our 20th anniversary. We spent the first morning eating breakfast on the beach and visiting the shops downtown. I thought it was unusual when my husband darted across the street and asked me to stop so he could snap my picture. I didn't get the full impact until I arrived home and picked up the prints from the lab. As Ricky Ricardo would say, he "had some 'splaining to do."

Laura Browne **Midland, Mich.**

Everyone knows a priest doesn't want a wife

As a young cleric in Rome, I ventured to purchase a sweater. I'd been studying Italian and decided I was ready for a test run. Dressed in my religious habit, I went to a clothing store in Trastevere. I told the young shopkeeper that I was there to buy a sweater, but instead of saying *maglia* (sweater), I said *moglie* (wife). She smiled and asked me what kind of *moglie* I'd like. A *moglie negra*, I said—a black wife. By that time a small group of women had gathered. She asked me to be more specific. I said I wanted a *pesante negra moglie*—a heavy black wife. The audience giggled. She then asked why I wanted a heavy black wife. "*Riscaldarmi*," I responded—to keep me warm. Everybody howled, and the shopkeeper told me in perfect English that she might not have a heavy black wife for me but she did happen to have a very nice sweater.

Philip Traynor **Fresno, Calif.**

Luckily, she *isn't* a pianist

When I flew to Lviv, Ukraine, my luggage didn't arrive with me. The following day my hostess, Olya, offered to take me to the airport to collect my bags. As we were getting into the van, I accidentally slammed her fingers in the door. Luckily, she's a physician, and her coworkers were able to sew up the wound in time for her to join me that night, as I had to catch a train. This time, she wisely held her bandaged hand close to her body as we got into the van, but somehow I slammed her other hand in the door! Now when I visit, we walk.

Ksenia Hapij Livingston, N.J.

La vie en yellow

During a bike trip to watch the Tour de France, my wife and I showed support for Lance Armstrong's foundation by wearing yellow bracelets, and we brought two more to hand out. On our final day we found a great B&B. Over dinner with the family who lived there, we learned that they were avid cyclists, and the next morning we presented the bracelets to the husband and wife. Their son told us that his mother was undergoing treatment for cancer, and she pointed to the wig that she'd been wearing all along. Her trembling hands put on the bracelet as she quietly said, "*Merci*." Our eyes filled with tears as hugs and best wishes were exchanged.

C. J. Pietrofesa **Lake Tahoe, Calif.**

Seaweed, indeed

My husband and I went fishing on a small boat while on Mexico's Riviera Maya. When we noticed a military helicopter hovering above with soldiers carrying machine guns, the boat owner said the soldiers were looking for drug dealers. I was the first to get a bite, and we were all excited to finally land a fish. "The big one" ended up being a large brick of marijuana; my hook had snagged the plastic it was wrapped in. Our captain was thrilled and kept telling us the parcel wasn't drugs. Having just seen the soldiers, we weren't looking forward to spending the rest of our lives in a Mexican prison, so we informed the captain that we wanted to throw it back. The captain spotted another boat and yelled to the fisherman—who quickly stripped off his clothes, swam over to our boat, and happily relieved us of our catch of the day.

Therese Buthod **Tulsa, Okla.**

"Cygnet Lake" just doesn't have the same ring to it

On a trip to Italy, my wife and I noticed a sign in Italian with three recognizable words: SWAN LAKE and TCHAIKOVSKY. Wanting to add some culture to our tour, we purchased tickets. After returning to the hotel and changing clothes, we ate at a local pizza place because we didn't want to miss the start of the show. We then entered the theater and were shown to excellent seats very close to the stage. Imagine our amazement when we saw that the entire cast was 4 and 5 years old. We'd bought tickets to a local dance studio's recital.

Edward Avadenka Bloomfield Hills, Mich.

Instamatic friendship

I was walking the streets of Rome when I heard a repeated roar of cheering at the Trevi Fountain. A harried young woman, laden with over two dozen cameras, was snapping one photo after another for her fellow travelers. I couldn't resist—I dashed over, handed her my camera, and plopped down right in the middle of the group. The fun-loving bunch loudly cheered once more. I never did find out who my 26 new best friends were, but their laughter was undeniably contagious.

Joan Brooks **Scottsdale, Ariz.**

You try doing it in high winds

My friend and I were in Buenos Aires, and our guidebook recommended Tierra Santa, a religious theme park that resembles Jerusalem. "We regret to inform you that Christ will not be resurrected due to high winds," said a voice over the loudspeaker as we entered. "We will resume the resurrection as soon as possible." Twenty minutes later the winds died down, and sure enough, an eight-foot-tall Jesus emerged from a mountain. "Ave Maria" played, and everyone stopped to watch.

Caroline Friesen Seattle, Wash.

Skip the second encore

Amid the ruins of Ollantaytambo, in Peru, a trio of girls stood waiting to sing us a song and pose for pictures. After the song was over, the littlest girl ran over to one of the huge terraces, squatted down, flipped up her colorful dress, and pooped!

Mary Lu and Charles Foreman Shawnee, Kans.

Like gloves would help

After a long day of traveling, I welcomed the delightfully clean bathroom in my quaint English B&B. Of course, I didn't need my glasses for a trip to the bathroom. I was pleased to see baby wipes on the back of the toilet, as I had forgotten to pack my own. They had a nice lemon scent. About three minutes later, I couldn't believe the sensation I was experiencing—then it hit me. I went back into the bathroom, this time with my glasses on. I had used a bathroom cleaning product that clearly stated, "Beware. Use of gloves is recommended."

Regina Pabo Independence, Ore.

What, no Murray Head?

One night in Bangkok, a friend and I stumbled into a bar. Only after ordering drinks did we notice it was a karaoke bar. I coaxed my friend into singing Madonna and Billy Joel, and the Thai crowd was pleased with her American accent. Then a waiter handed us a slip of paper, with ONEWAYORANOTHER written on it. A request! We began singing the Blondie hit, and the dance floor filled with locals mouthing the words. We encored with "Y.M.C.A."

Jen Abraczinskas **Catawissa, Pa.**

And they probably had some cute little word for it

One night in Henley-on-Thames, England, my boyfriend and I went to a tapas restaurant. There was a terra-cotta dish on the table. Wondering what it was, I picked it up and saw that it had liquid in it. Richard dunked his fingers, tasted them, and declared that it was oil for dipping bread. Then he said it might be a finger bowl. So we asked the waitress, who told us it was an ashtray.

Kristen Bergevin Los Angeles, Calif.

Arf, barf

During one of the lengthy bus trips on our tour of China, we stopped at a nondescript store for a bathroom break. I wandered outside, where an elderly gentleman had a small stand selling snacks. Fond of beef jerky, I spotted something that looked delectable. I smiled and said, "Moo, moo?" He shook his head and answered, "Bowwow!"

Jane O'Brien Savannah, Ga.

Who says you have to choose?

Before I left on a Gate 1 trip to Peru, my friend Janis warned me to be careful around any llamas. "I've heard they spit on you and it's really nasty," she said. At a llama farm near Cuzco, I had no trouble with the llamas or the alpacas. A vicuña, however, bit me and tried to give me a good thrashing with his hooves. I believe I'd rather be spit on if I had to choose between the two.

Marlene Jackson Columbus, Ind.

Hey, it's Robin Williams!

I had just entered a museum in Riga, Latvia, when I saw this long-haired guy at a computer, watching a slide show of prehistoric cave paintings. I went to tell him that prehistoric art was a major interest of mine, but as I began to talk, I realized that he wasn't a regular guy, but a life-size replica of a Paleolithic caveman! He was wrapped in animal skins and clicking away at a mouse. I managed to regain my composure, then took out my camera.

Sarah Pearlman West Hartford, Conn.

The difference between snorkeling and skin diving

During our honeymoon on Bora-Bora, my husband and I went snorkeling with a group. A cameraman was supposed to be filming the group, but he kept following me. Back on land we purchased the DVD, figuring it'd be mostly of us. When we got home, we invited our family over to watch it. To everyone's surprise, my swimsuit top had evidently suffered a wardrobe malfunction—which explains why the cameraman was fascinated with me.

Melissa O'Halloran **Yonkers, N.Y.**

You're a perfect 12

My friend and I took the bus while traveling from Kuşadasi to Istanbul, in Turkey. Once on board, he struck up a conversation with the friendly attendant, who spoke limited English. At the end of the five-hour journey, the attendant told my friend where he lived and what time we should be at his house. Confused, I told him we were sorry, but we'd be leaving Turkey soon. He shook his head and said, "Man make me very good trade," pointing to me and smiling. "Ten sheep, two goat." While I was sleeping, my buddy had apparently sold me for some livestock. My friend and I looked at each other for an uncomfortable moment, until the young man finally laughed and let us off the hook.

Christeen Pozniak **West Palm Beach, Fla.**

Those quotation marks are making us uncomfortable

Some people travel with pets, but I bring my "kids": five stuffed animals that I leave on the hotel bed when my boyfriend and I are out exploring. While we were in Boston, our housekeeper left them in different and interesting "poses" after cleaning the room. We enjoyed going back to our hotel each night to find what "poses" our kids were in. Our housekeeper definitely made the trip unforgettable!

Yi-Miao Huang Flushing, N.Y.

Well, it *is* easier to spell

While in the Czech Republic, my husband and I drove to a small city called Český Krumlov, where we checked into the Hotel Renesance. The next day we visited the castle, tasted the cuisine, and sampled local beers. As a matter of fact, we did a pretty good pub crawl before calling it a night. Try as we might, however, we couldn't find our hotel. We thought we knew where it was, but the only place that resembled the Hotel Renesance was named Leonardo. After four trips around the block, we went up to the door and tried our key. It worked! While we were cavorting around the city, the Hotel Renesance was given a new name!

Carol Banning San Pedro, Calif.

Cheesaholics Anonymous, we have a pickup for you

My friend Sarah and I love to say that we "cheesed" our way around France. Each morning, we looked forward to selecting cheeses for lunch, generally a stinky one and then something milder and creamy. On our last day, in Paris, we took our cheese to the Ile de la Cité. On a bench in dappled sunlight, we feasted. There was a heat wave, so it wasn't surprising when the couple across from us moved over to the shade. As we left, we commended their wisdom in retreating from the sun. It turns out that they were driven from their seats not by the heat, but by the odor of our cheese!

Gillian Ward Kingston, Ont.

Prince Eric is in for a shock

We went to visit Copenhagen's Little Mermaid sculpture, but she wasn't anywhere to be found—she had been blown up the night before we arrived. I bought a souvenir sculpture from a kiosk and shot a picture of it on the rock. The replica was terribly unsatisfying, so I scrambled onto the rock and posed for a photo—everyone, including people on tour boats passing by, laughed and applauded.

Scott Ashkenaz Palo Alto, Calif.

More like the Inebriateds

I had a fantastic time in Iceland, made even better by an impromptu encounter with the Incredibles. Well, not the real Incredibles, but graduating high school students inspired by the film to don snappy uniforms and display feats of gymnastic daring. I caught them striking a heroic team pose.

Michael Sacarny Arlington, Mass.

Never been to Akron, eh?

My friend Carlos and I were barhopping around Amsterdam when we met some Americans who insisted that we check out the Stablemaster bar. Their excitement sparked our curiosity, so we went there. The door was locked. I rang the bell, and a gentleman opened the door a few inches and peered out with one eye. "What do you want?" he asked. I responded that we were there to visit the bar. He informed us that there was a cover charge, then reluctantly let us in. When we walked inside, we were stunned. He was naked except for his shoes. In fact, everyone was naked. It was "naked night," which included happy-hour drink specials. He handed us plastic bags for our clothes, but we quickly left. Apparently, Dutch happy hour is a little different than it is in Ohio.

Richard Resatka Columbus, Ohio

He might have meant both

Having endured a sleepless flight to Iceland, my daughter and I checked in to our hotel and began making plans to explore Reykjavík. We signed up for a trip to the Blue Lagoon later that day, thinking that the mineral-rich water would soothe our tired bodies. When we finally got on the bus, we were dragging from lack of sleep. I was nodding off when we arrived a half hour later, but I woke up in a hurry when the guide said that our dip in the lagoon would be especially good for our eczema and our sorry asses. After a collective gasp from the crowd, we figured out that he meant psoriasis.

Susan Poirier Windsor, Conn.

A nun with a whip doesn't need a funny headline

On a motorcycle trip through the Alps, my friend Bill and I stopped for lunch at a café in Ponte di Legno, a village in northern Italy. It was a local hangout with lively conversation, great food, and even a guitar-carrying nun. After we sat down, we noticed people beginning to file outside, followed by a series of loud noises. "Are those firecrackers?" Bill asked. I looked out the window, and I couldn't believe my eyes. The nun, all of five feet tall, was cracking a bullwhip to the cheers of the crowd. With her feet planted, habit flying, and whip snapping, she ought to have been in a rodeo!

David A. Sweze **Everett, Wash.**

First candy from strangers, and now this

A friendly gentleman approached me while I was touring Paracas, Peru, with my mother. He was selling candy on the beach, and as I was choosing some candy, he invited me to his home to meet the family pet—a penguin. A little hesitant, but curious, I followed him down the street, around the corner, and through several alleys. Upon entering his home I was warmly greeted by the family and introduced to their pride and joy, a pet penguin!

Christy Bowie Jacksonville, Fla.

Rubbed the wrong way

Concerned about offending the locals in Thailand, my friend and I bought a guidebook about the country's rituals and customs. Upon arrival, we wanted a massage, and the concierge booked us an appointment at the hotel. Our petite therapist instructed us to remove our tops. She sat behind me—not too strange for my Western blood—but then she grabbed me around the waist. "I love American girl," she said. "You have big boobies." She proceeded to jiggle them. To think, we were worried about offending people.

Nicole Barker Costa Mesa, Calif.

We'll be darned if that camel isn't having a Coke and a smile

I came across a man with his camel near one of the major tourist sites in Petra, Jordan. He pointed at the soda bottle I was holding, so I gave it to him. He took a drink, then gave the rest to his camel, which held the bottle in its mouth and finished every last drop! I was ready to retrieve a beer from my hotel for the camel's next trick, but the man said that his camel doesn't drink on the job.

Adam Tennen Scottsdale, Ariz.

Just peel and eat

After spending two months in Africa, my husband and I invited my 20-year-old nephew to visit us in Malawi. Having never left his little town in Texas, he jumped at the chance. We picked him up at the airport, complete with his macho attitude. After we stowed his luggage in the car, we told him we'd stop for a snack on the way home. My nephew, hungry from his long flight, was all for it. All the macho left him, however, when my hubby pulled over to buy a few dried mice from the guy who sells them on the road outside the airport. (We called them mice jerky.) This trip was certainly an eye-opening experience for our little Texan.

Jennifer Martines **Los Lunas, N.M.**

Never lift the mattress

In the countryside near Golfito, Costa Rica, I spent the night in an open-air thatched hut. My bed was a mattress on a wooden pallet raised a few feet above the ground. It was surprisingly comfortable, and the mosquito netting protected me from bugs, bats, and other flying critters. In the morning, however, I noticed that several ants were hiking up one of the bed's legs. I lifted the mattress: There was a colony of thousands of ants tending saucer-size clusters of ant eggs.

John B. Kachuba Athens, Ohio

His name: Pepé Le Pew

While in Paris, I took an evening cruise on the Seine. The cruise was very peaceful until I felt a hot tongue on my neck. The guy next to me had licked me! I turned to him and said, "Excuse me, what the hell are you doing?" "Hey, baby, it's okay. I just wanted to see how you be tasting," he replied. Talk about the city of love!

Danielle D. Grimm **Rochester, N.Y.**

Here's a twenty if it'll help

In the Hanoi airport on our way home, my friend said she had put her spare currency in the charity box. Since I had no use for my leftover dong, I went to check out the box. It left me speechless.

Stacy Friedman **New York, N.Y.**

Now playing: *Dracula on Vacation* (rated PG-13)

In Puerto Vallarta, Mexico, my friends and I stopped at a bar. It was my friend's birthday, so I privately asked the waitress if they do anything special. "Oh yes," she said. When we were done eating, the waitresses sang "Happy Birthday" and told the birthday boy he'd get free shots if he'd sit on the bar. He got up on the bar, and they quickly put a rope around his ankles, hoisted him into the air, and spun him around after each shot.

Jenny Mashek Curtis, Nebr.

The merman of Venice

My wife and I arrived at the Venice airport only to discover that my bag didn't make it. On our third and final morning in the city, I was sitting on our balcony when I spotted a gondola bringing my bag down the canal. The gondola docked in front of my hotel, and a man on board tried to lift my luggage onto a walkway—but instead he dropped it into the water! I ran downstairs and shouted at him, but he simply flashed me an I-don't-know-what-you're-talking-about look. After frantically waving euros, I found a young guy who took off his shoes and shirt, dove in, and got my bag. The hotel washed and dried everything in just a few hours, and we were off to Florence.

James Goodwin Ponte Vedra Beach, Fla.

Since cows are female, that makes you transvestites

I've got 10 friends who travel a lot, and we have an ongoing contest to see who can have the most pictures taken of us wearing cow suits in foreign countries. At the Yachana Lodge in Ecuador, two of us managed to get a good shot with the staff. When we were leaving the country, however, the customs officer opened my bag, and out popped an udder. He rolled his eyes as I stood there with a sheepish—or cowish?—grin. From now on, the cow suit is definitely going in my carry-on!

Pete Skinner Tallahassee, Fla.

Scarlett O'Hara in Bhutan

My first purchase while I was in Bhutan was an embroidered tablecloth. It was the perfect size for my dining room table. The day after I bought it, my traveling companions and I were lucky enough to be invited to a wedding. We needed proper attire and asked our guide where to buy a dress. "You bought a dress yesterday!" he said, confused. My new tablecloth was actually a Bhutanese dress. They look beautiful on the women of Bhutan, but I'm afraid they didn't do much for us!

Roxanne Lippel Los Angeles, Calif.

Jehovah's Witnesses?

At a hotel in Suzhou, China, my parents and I were awakened by a late-night telephone call. "Yes?" my mother answered groggily. "You have a message?" A pause. "Of course, what is it?" The caller's English was poor, and my mother didn't know what the message could possibly be. Soon afterward, there was a knock at our door. Through the peephole, I saw two women in miniskirts and heavy eye shadow. "You want massage?" asked one. Needless to say, I turned the women away, explaining to my parents exactly whom my mother had invited to our room.

Brian Edstrom **St. Paul, Minn.**

You'd hate Brazil

As an ordinary, but quite hairy, West Coast girl, I jumped at the opportunity for a five-day trip to Bali with my best friend. On the first day, at the Tanah Lot temple, three men asked if they could take a photo with me. Hesitantly, I accepted. They quickly swarmed around, nuzzling me. Two days later, our concierge asked if he could stroke my arm and leg, and on day four, a man in traditional clothing tried to kiss me! On our final day, a taxi driver explained that body hair is a sign of femininity in Bali and that most men find it sexy. He said I'm like a goddess— the men would build me altars and give me daily offerings and I'd never have to do anything again. My next trip to Bali is already in the works.

Megan Schutt **Blaine, Wash.**

Likely story

"Wait!" I said, rolling my eyes. "You're taking me to fire water?" My Jamaican host, iTall, insisted that yes, indeed he was. "Water can't be on fire," I protested. "It would put itself out." Wonders never cease: That afternoon, I lit, touched, and soaked in a magical pool of dancing flames—a mineral spring fed by waters that release flammable gases.

Melissa Sapio **New York, N.Y.**

"Dude, the things they do with olive oil will blow your mind"

While in Las Vegas on business, I was telling my associates about the great tapas place we'd gone to the night before. We talked about the variety of dishes offered and how the service was also good. Overhearing our conversation, one of my other friends announced that he'd had a great night as well. He said that he had gone to a place even better than ours, that he'd gotten to know the owner, and that the bouncers were very discreet. He also mentioned that the assortment was spectacular and that every woman in the place was beautiful. It wasn't until he'd been speaking awhile that we realized he thought we'd gone to a *topless* place.

Brad Lee Reno, Nev.

Too much bathtub gin?

My mother and my aunt weren't about to let their age stop them from relishing every mile of their Cosmos tour to Europe. The pair of octogenarians took part in every single activity and enjoyed the friendship of their much younger tour companions. And after a day spent touring the Vatican proved too much for her tired, aching feet, my mom even improvised a refreshing spa treatment.

Merry Noel Reed Portland, Ore.

Cherchez la fembot

At Expo 2005 in Japan, robots were everywhere. The best ones were the multilingual information-bots programmed to answer questions about the event. These robots looked, acted, and talked like real women. "You're very beautiful," I said to one. "Will you marry me?" Expecting her to tell me that she was programmed to only give information and advice about Expo, I couldn't believe her response: "Underneath these clothes I have a beautiful body. But I cannot take them off here."

Bruce Klahr Boulder, Colo.

Hand it to the folks on the other side of the curtain

My son and I traveled to St. Thomas, in the U.S. Virgin Islands, when he was 4 years old. On each of our flights, we studied the pocket card to review the plane's safety features. We focused on the picture that read, DO NOT THROW ANYTHING DOWN THE TOILET. I explained to my son why this was an important rule. Ten days later, on our way home, we again reviewed the safety card on each flight. On our final leg, my son went to the lavatory. Some time had passed when the flight attendant approached me with a horrified look. "He needs you!" she said. My son was behind her, holding up a wad of decidedly used toilet paper. "What am I supposed to do with this?" he asked.

John Larson **Dorchester, Mass.**

Everybody has one

My husband and I were fishing in Australia with the assistance of a Canadian guide. I asked if we were fishing in an area with puffer fish—and just as he replied in the affirmative, I felt a tug on my line. I reeled it in, and, believe it or not, it was a puffer. It wasn't the first time I'd caught a puffer fish. The first time, I explained to the group, I hadn't hooked it in the mouth but rather in the bunghole. Our guide, puzzled, asked if that was our "secret fishing place."

Myrt Klukas **Omaha, Nebr.**

Good thing for you you're never going to age

To celebrate my 40th birthday and my mother's 70th, we went to England to see exactly where our ancestors lived. After a week of driving on the wrong side of the road, we were on the wrong side of each other's nerves. Then we got turned around on a roundabout and became lost somewhere in the Cotswolds. I spotted this sign and informed my mom that this was her stop.

Tricia Du Four Twin Peaks, Calif.

Hey, it never hurts to ask

Years ago, my parents were on a trip in Mexico that involved a long bus ride. Midway through, the Mexican tour leader said in a loud voice, "Would anyone like to get out and spread their legs?"

Patricia Holbrook Santa Fe, N.M.

That'll clear things up

I was volunteering at a wildlife sanctuary in South Africa when the resident monkey, a vervet named Monk-kay, became playful with me. He'd focus on the inside of my mouth, sometimes even banging his teeth against mine. When I returned home, I went to my dentist for a checkup. The hygienist asked about the scrapes in my mouth. "Oh, that was just Monk-kay digging around in my mouth," I said. The hygienist gave me a look and scribbled in my chart. The dentist came in and looked at my chart. "What's this about a monkey in your mouth?" he said. Next time I'll have to bring the photos!

Stacey Potthier Minneapolis, Minn.

Score one for the llama

My fiancée and I enjoy zoos and animal parks. While at a park in Bandon, Ore., I got to spend some one-on-one time with a llama. I was stroking his neck, and he seemed to be enjoying it, when— *wham!* I was covered from head to waist with the most vile-smelling vomit I've ever known. It was in my hair, on my clothes, even in my mouth and up my nose. As I stood there dumbfounded, wondering what happened, my fiancée was doubled over laughing. She evidently knew that llamas are known to spit—but she failed to clue me in until it was too late. To this day I suffer from llamaphobia.

Richard Kyle **Bellevue, Wash.**

We just wish
we'd thought of it

I hopped into a phone booth in London to call home. The next thing I knew, two boys were circling the phone booth, wrapping it in duct tape! Then they ran away, squealing with laughter, leaving me humiliated and trapped. I had to wait quite some time for a passerby to free me. Trying to regain my dignity as I headed down the street, I saw the boys lurking in an alleyway. They were smiling and waving, and I couldn't help but smile back. It seems good old childhood pranks know no borders.

Stephanie Fallon West Chester, Pa.

Pandora's tacos

I was in Mazatlán, Mexico, for the first time, when my husband took me to what he said was the best roadside taco stand. I love to be adventurous, and so I ordered two—one taco *de la cabeza* (cow's head) and one taco *de la lengua* (tongue). On the first bite of the tongue taco, I bit into what felt like a rock. I spit it out. It looked like a tooth. No, it *was* a tooth—and not one of mine. I calmly put the taco down, trying not to upset the cook, who stood right across from me, beaming with pride. Yikes! The smile had a gap. I may have been brave enough to try the tacos, but I wasn't brave enough to find out if the cook was the original owner of my find.

May Morrisroe **Atascadero, Calif.**

What an ass

It was dawn when my tour group arrived at the Nile River to choose our donkeys for a ride to the Valley of the Kings. There must have been more than 100 milling around and I, at almost five feet nine inches tall, was most concerned about the height of my donkey—I didn't want my feet to drag on the ground. "Madame, may I assist you?" asked an older Egyptian man in flowing robes. I explained that I was searching for a tall donkey. He looked me up and down. "Madame," he replied, "may I suggest that you look for a strong donkey?"

Patricia Quinones **St. Louis, Mo.**

A filthy story

In Guanacaste, Costa Rica, my husband, Scott, and I hurried back from a hike to make it in time for our mud bath. The other guests were already coated in mud and baking in the sun. When we entered the hut, two men motioned for Scott to leave while they studiously painted me from head to toe, leaving no skin uncovered, and following close around my bikini. When I emerged, the people in our group asked how I got my mud on so perfectly; theirs was streaky and uneven. I said that was how the two men applied it. "What men?" they said. "We were all told to put it on ourselves!" Scott and I never did see those two guys again.

Pam Anderson Sussex, Wis.

Don't go chasing skirts if you can't handle the consequences

While studying abroad in London, a few girlfriends and I came across a group of burly rugby players in a pub. They were all wearing kilts and partying quite wildly. My friend bet me that they didn't wear underwear—then she went right over and asked them. The entire team flashed us simultaneously. Well, we definitely got our answer.

Laurie Johns Reno, Nev.

There's a rugby player in London who could use them

On our last day in Vienna before going to Rome, my husband, daughter, and I were almost out of clean clothes. We had just enough time to run into a laundromat, where a nice elderly man helped us figure out the machines. Against our protests, he even took his laundry out of the dryer early, so we wouldn't have to wait. We told the good man we wouldn't forget his kindness and dashed for the station. Once we'd settled into our compartment, we started sorting our clean clothes and realized we had something else to remember him by.

Maria Goodavage **San Francisco, Calif.**

No double-dipping!

As an expat in London, I often noticed strange signs. The best was in an elegant apothecary in Eton, outside Windsor. Imagine my surprise when, perusing their lotions, I spotted this jar of ointment.

Lisa Hughet **Raleigh, N.C.**

Caught between a rock and a hard place

At a B&B in Killinick, Ireland, my father decided to take a short walk around the gardens. I followed and could see him standing in front of a statue. As I approached, he bent over to have a look, and, without laughing, I grabbed my camera just as he reached out for further inspection. The caption in my photo album now reads, "Touch that again, old man, and you'll find out why I'm frowning."

Linda Coates **Colorado Springs, Colo.**

Regional atrocity is more like it

My friend and I often bought cheese, bread, and olives to enjoy for lunch while in Sardinia. One day we were having a picnic when my friend shrieked and pointed to the cheese—there were maggots in it! That same night, at dinner with a local family, we told the story, and the husband roared with laughter. He asked his wife to bring out their cheese and then dug a spoon into the middle. It came out full of cheese and maggots. He put the cheese in his mouth and explained that it was a regional delicacy.

Ries Wichers Cambridge, Mass.

The kids dress better, too

In a hill-tribe village in northern Thailand, where women smoke pipes, chickens run rampant, and children attend an open-air school with mats on the ground instead of desks, my friend asked my 6-year-old son, "It sure is different from Portland, isn't it?" "Yeah," he replied. "It's sunny here."

Rudy Barton Portland, Ore.

Or maybe the thief was keeping kosher

My husband and I adored Vieques, Puerto Rico—especially Porkchop, a stray dog who followed us all over. On our third night, we awoke to hair-raising barking outside our guesthouse's door. There was a burglar in the living room! The intruder ran off with my husband's wallet and camera, but thanks to Porkchop, he didn't make it down the hall to our bedroom. Porkchop saved us, and we knew we had to return the favor. We waited months while he recovered from heartworm treatment at the Vieques Humane Society. Now he's at home with us, adjusting well to the change in climate.

Sarah Svindland **Laconia, N.H.**

She prefers Tanqueray

Because I was six months pregnant, I was cautious about sampling wine on a trip I took to Italy with my husband and 3-year-old daughter. At a Montalcino winery, we told the steward I didn't need a glass, but he came back with two glasses anyway. We politely re-informed him that I didn't need one. He said he understood and put a glass in front of my daughter. We told him she wouldn't be tasting either. "She does not drink wine?" he said, amazed.

Sharon Bryant Knoxville, Tenn.

Too much Molson, eh?

I stopped to watch the changing of the guard in Ottawa. The sun was beating down, and I thought about how hot it must be in those bearskin hats. Suddenly, a guard in the back row spat. I kept my eye on him as he spat several more times. Then he spewed a river of vomit, and—maintaining his posture—he fell backward like a nutcracker. The crowd gasped, but not a soldier flinched, nor did anyone dare to interrupt to assist the man. The ceremony proceeded as if nothing had happened, until finally, a commander signaled for two medics to carry the soldier away on a stretcher.

Pam Wendler-Shaw **Charlottesville, Va.**

You know, like
Michael Jackson

Last winter, I volunteered with Global Crossroad in
Tanzania, teaching orphans and underprivileged
children in a preschool. When I ran out of clean
pants, I wore my daughter's skirt—it was a bit short
for me so I wore black nylons underneath. When I
entered the classroom, I got strange looks from the
kids, and they rubbed their hands all over my legs.
Everyone was laughing! Afterward, a teacher told
me that the children thought that I was half black
and half white. They had never seen nylons before.

Jeannine Williamson **Fritz Creek, Alaska**

The moral: Hold your bananas elsewhere

At the caves in Phang Nga, Thailand, a large adult monkey wanted the bananas I was carrying. I tried to break one off, but it wouldn't budge. The monkey grew impatient and excited. The harder I tried, the more perturbed the monkey became—until he finally grabbed my manhood! He held on while growling and showing his teeth. My mind went blank, paralyzed with fear. A crowd formed as I danced around with this monkey attached to me. Eventually, it occurred to me to just throw him the whole bunch of bananas. As he ran off, I turned to see that I was the star of quite a few home videos.

Thomas White Palmer, Alaska

Or so he told Aunt Edith

Years ago my Aunt Edith and Uncle Frank won a Windjammer Barefoot Cruise. Though already in their eighties, they thoroughly enjoyed vacationing with a much younger and more active set. Early in the cruise, Frank was waiting by the mast for my aunt when a young, attractive, and topless woman accosted him for staring—she cursed him up one side and down the other. When Edith finally arrived and was able to stop laughing, she explained to the woman that Frank was legally blind.

Kent Millwood **Belton, S.C.**

Let's hear it!

On our cruise ship, my niece and I kept bumping into one couple. When I finally approached them, they burst out laughing. "We've been following you," the man said. "You're always saying funny things that we can send to *Budget Travel*'s True Stories."

Gustava Phillips Berryville, Ark.

Got a good travel story?

Send it to us! In every issue of *Budget Travel* magazine, we give the best story a terrific prize (usually a trip). All of the details, including contest guidelines, can be found at BudgetTravel.com/TrueStories.

Thanks again to everyone who ever submitted a story, and in particular to the folks whose stories are in this book. We couldn't have done it without you!

We're also grateful to all the folks who had a hand in creating this book, including (at *Budget Travel*) designers Sarah Irick and Jacky Carter, assistant editor David LaHuta, copy editor Thomas Berger, attorney Randy Shapiro, and our book agent Bruce Harris. And finally, thanks to the marvelous team at Andrews McMeel, including editor Patty Rice, assistant editor Katie Anderson, copy chief Michelle Daniel, production editor Caty Neis, and cover designer RenWhei Harn.